My
Law of
Attraction
Project Planner

Pamela Thompson
Donna Hawkins

With Tools for Creating
Abundance, Success, and Joy

My Law of Attraction Project Planner

Published by Pamela Thompson and Donna Hawkins
ISBN-13: 978-1535037846 / ISBN-10: 1535037849

SCAN HERE with your cell phone's free QR Reader app
to go directly to Pamela Thompson's Author Page on Amazon.
There, you will find a Supplement to this book, and other Law of Attraction
coloring books and journals to further assist you with lining up your energy
and becoming a match to your desires.

Before First Use

We urge you to read through this entire Project Planner prior to your first project,
and make use of all the practice spaces provided,
in order to get the utmost benefit from all the tools and information herein.

Supplement Now Available

If you would like to continue to do your deliberate planning in a bound book,
our *Supplement to My Law of Attraction Project Planner* is now available on Amazon,
or by scanning the QR code on the opposite page. The Supplement contains
3 additional months of Daily Tools sheets, 12 extra sets of Project Plan sheets,
12 68-Seconds of Pure Positive Focus sheets, and 3 Celebrating My Successes sheets.

Please help us out by leaving a review on Amazon.

Thank you!

"Every 25 Reviews" Drawing

Please "Like" our Facebook page – *My Law of Attraction Project Planner* – to continue to be inspired, and to enjoy reading the success stories of others and adding your own.

Message us through this page as soon as you've left us a review on Amazon, providing a link to your review or your specific Amazon name so we can confirm it, in order to be eligible for the next drawing.

For every 25 confirmed reviews we receive on Amazon, there will be a drawing for a free copy of our *Supplement to My Law of Attraction Project Planner.*

CONTENTS

There is no way to Happiness.

Happiness is the way.

Bring Happiness to all that you do.

If you advance confidently in the direction of your own dreams, and endeavor to live the life which you have imagined, you will meet with a success unexpected in common hours. Your imagination is your greatest gift. Anything that you can place into your imagination can harden into a reality.

~ Wayne Dyer[1] ~

[1] From a compilation of Wayne Dyer's inspirational messages, "Visualization TV - Imagine Your Wildest Dreams". Visualization TV. N.p., 2016. Web. April 9, 2016.

INTRO

Plan Daily Projects or Life Change Projects

This Project Planner will be useful for just about anything you want to give positive momentum to –

> ➤ Your plans for a particular day's events
> ➤ Upcoming projects with many steps
> ➤ Major life events such as moving, finding a new job, or planning a wedding
> ➤ Deliberately attracting anything you want to be, do, or have into your reality

The tools and processes we've provided will help you accomplish any project with much greater ease, and allow you to organize and complete each one more efficiently and effectively. Your life will go more smoothly, and you will attract more and more of your desired outcomes.

Why Use the Law of Attraction with a Project Planner?

As you will come to see (if you don't already know), understanding how the Law of Attraction works, and learning to use it to your benefit while organizing your life, can make all the difference in the world in what you create. This is because *your thoughts actually create your reality.* They vibrate on frequencies, just like sound waves and radio waves, and they attract vibrations of the same frequencies for every different thing you focus on, in every moment.

As you continue to think about certain subjects, and talk about them with others, your thoughts attract more and more similar thoughts, and eventually "become" your reality. This is how the Law of Attraction ("like" attracts "like") operates. It's a Universal Law that affects your life, whether you acknowledge it or not, just as the Law of Gravity does.

Therefore, you can create the reality you desire – not by action alone, as you've been trained to believe – but by focusing *most* of your thoughts on what you *want*, rather than obsessing over what you don't want. Unfortunately, thinking about the negative side of things rather than the positive (whatever we want instead) is what we humans usually do. We've become very good at it over the course of our lifetimes, and it's a hard habit to break. But if you want to enjoy a *better feeling life*, you need to learn how to *feel better now*, by training your thoughts.

This Project Planner will help you train your thoughts with a series of easy-to-use, very effective tools. The tools will help you become accustomed to thinking positively more often than negatively, and help you plan the life you want with unbelievable ease. You will become what Abraham refers to as a "deliberate creator" and what we call a *"deliberate planner!"*

Deliberate Planning

"Reactive planning" is the way we've all been taught to use planners – we fill the calendar and to-do list portions with appointments based on things that "come up." Every single thing we write in these planners is based on our reaction to something life throws us. Wanted or unwanted, it's all reaction-based. These planners are simply chronicles of the decisions we make as a result of our reactions.

"Deliberate Planning," as opposed to reactive planning, is the purpose of this Project Planner.

Deliberate planning is simply deciding what you want, and intentionally putting yourself in a position to receive it, once you understand how the Law of Attraction works. Unlike reactive planning, this approach requires more than merely entering appointments and adding to your list of things to do. As you will see below, it requires you to do whatever it takes to succeed with Step 3, which is not at all easy for most of us, at first. We've all been trained, practically from birth, to look at things from a negative perspective. The variety of tools included in this Project Planner will help you start to see things differently, so that you can act more *knowingly.*

These are the 3 Steps to using the Law of Attraction *deliberately:*

1. <u>Ask</u> – You already do this all of the time, often without realizing it. Any time you have a desire, which is naturally in the form of thoughts, you are asking. *Now, you're going to learn to become more aware of what you're asking for, and how to properly identify anything that you want to deliberately create for your future.*

2. <u>Answer</u> – The Universe . . . Source . . . God . . . your Inner Being . . . whomever you consider your Higher Power . . . "hears" your thoughts vibrationally, and makes the object of your desire *available* to you. You don't have to worry about this step at all.

    So, you can see that the first two steps are a piece of cake. Once you learn to train your thoughts *adequately* regarding any particular desire, the third step will be easy, as well.

3. <u>Allow Yourself to Receive</u> – Remember, the Universe has already (in Step 2) made the essence of your desire available – at a vibrational level, or pre-manifestation level. Now, your responsibility is to train your thoughts to vibrate highly enough (positively enough) to *match the frequency of your desire,* in order to attract it in your life.

Matching the high frequency of your desire, in its current non-physical, vibrational, pure energy form, simply means reaching the point, and maintaining it, where the majority of your thoughts about your desire are good feeling thoughts. There are many ways to do this, as you will see.

But if your thoughts vibrate on frequencies, like sound waves and radio waves, and you obviously can't see them or read them on a dial, how can you tell whether they're attaining a frequency high enough to attract what you want?

Fortunately, your emotions tell you whether your current thoughts on a subject are vibrating positively or negatively. In other words, they tell you what you're attracting in that moment with respect to that subject. Abraham refers to your emotions as your Guidance System. Ask yourself, in any given moment, how you're feeling right now. You don't even have to be able to put it into words or identify the emotion – is it positive or negative?

So, first and foremost, train yourself to pay close attention to your emotions!

When you become aware that you're not feeling positive, make a conscious effort to identify what's bugging you – and then, *as quickly as possible* – identify what you'd rather be experiencing instead, along with how you'd like to be feeling.

These moments or periods of contrast (things you don't want) are actually good, in a sense, because they provide you with a great deal more clarity about what it is that you actually want in your life. Once you're clear, your real work begins – deliberate planning.

Choosing and Using the Tools

There are many ways to become an emotional match to your desires – expressing appreciation or gratitude, focusing specifically on how you choose to feel using visualization, making manifestation boards with pictures or words representing what you want, meditating, and just plain having fun – these and others described in the next section will allow you to attract more of everything that feels good to you, since they will positively raise your vibration. The point is to find ways to allow yourself to feel as happy as if you've already attracted what you wish to be, do, or have. After all, the only reason we ever desire anything in the first place is because we believe we'll feel better once we have it. Why wait?

So, your main "job" is to feel as good as you can in any given moment.

We strongly encourage daily use of some tools, but the others may be used when it feels appropriate to you. We've included the "important" tools in the One Month to Positive Outcomes section to help you develop the habit of using them consistently to build up positive momentum for the day. This will enable you to attract more positive opportunities and outcomes. We encourage you to get up 20 minutes earlier if you need to, so you'll have time to do them first thing in the morning. In the long run, they will save you a lot of time because you will have lined up your energy and will be a match to attracting positive opportunities and outcomes with greater ease.

Being proactive in creating a higher vibration will allow you to be more open to Universal nudges and to take inspired action to attract your desires throughout the day with greater ease. You'll find that, when taking inspired action, you are much more productive than when you act just because you think you "should." You'll also be pleasantly surprised at the things you attract without having to take any action at all!

My Tools

Daily Tools

Appreciation/Gratitude List[2]

When you start off each day writing an Appreciation/Gratitude List, focusing on big or small things that you enjoy in your life right now, it automatically makes you feel good, or at least better. The most important thing is to keep it totally positive, because you get what you focus on, wanted or unwanted.

For example if you write, "I really appreciate the fact that my boss wasn't impatient yesterday," you're still focusing on your boss' impatience, and feeling the angst of that behavior. So, unless you raise your vibration in this area, you'll continue to attract unwanted behavior from your boss, or something else that feels as badly. A better feeling way to write it would be, "I really appreciate my boss being much more patient yesterday, and how well we got along." That definitely feels much better, and has greater potential for attracting continued ease with your boss, or other positive outcomes.

Include small things in your Appreciation/Gratitude Lists, not just big ones. Even expressing appreciation for dry towels after your shower, or for a hot cup of tea, will help you build positive momentum for your day. The happier you feel, and the longer you can continue positive momentum during your day, the better day you will have!

Example:

I really appreciate:

1. The gorgeous, sunny day I woke up to!
2. The restful sleep I had.
3. Finding a great mechanic for my car yesterday.
4. The delicious salads that the local general store makes.
5. My good health.
6. The internet.

Practice writing an Appreciation/Gratitude List on the next page. We suggest writing 6 things a day on this list, and making every day's list different.

---

[2] While Abraham typically uses the words "appreciation" and "appreciate," feel free to substitute "gratitude" and "grateful" if they are more a match to you.

I really appreciate:

1. _____

2. _____

3. _____

4. _____

5. _____

6. _____

Appreciation/Gratitude Intentions List

Your next Appreciation/Gratitude List should contain things you're focused on attaining, and you should state them as if you have them already. These are things you *intend* to attract, things you *choose* to enjoy. Make sure to word them in a positive manner, by describing what you want, instead of what you don't want. Writing them down will help you focus on them long enough to practice feeling as though you already have them. Over time, this will make you a vibrational match to your desires or other positive outcomes.

As you list your intentions, take several moments to visualize or imagine having them already – try to imagine how that would make you feel. Allow yourself to enjoy and milk those good feelings.

This tool may seem silly, since you don't have the items on the list yet. It's like playing pretend, but many of us are adults and we've been indoctrinated to "face reality." Well, the reality is that you create your own reality, and this is a very effective and fun way to do it.

If you feel any negativity trying to list your desires as if you have them already, try prefacing your list with "Wouldn't it be nice if," or "I intend to," or "I choose to," or "What if it was easy to," instead of "I really appreciate." Eventually, you will reprogram your conscious mind to actually believe that your desires are your future reality, and you'll be able to begin listing new desires much more comfortably as things you are already appreciative of.

You'll soon be amazed at how powerful this tool really is, and how powerful a creator you really are. So, make daily lists of what you *intend* to be, do, or have, and have fun doing it!

Example:

I really appreciate:

1. My favorite plant being very healthy and thriving.
2. My boss showing me mutual respect.
3. Feeling in control in all situations.
4. The great salary I'm making, and fantastic benefits! I can easily afford to pay my bills on time and have enough for fun.
5. Enjoying my time with my children.
6. My knee feeling great today, and the wonderful walk I took to the park and back.

Practice writing a Appreciation/Gratitude Intentions List on the next page. We suggest writing 6 things a day on this list, and making every day's list different.

I really appreciate:

1. _____

2. _____

3. _____

4. _____

5. _____

6. _____

Positive Aspects List

Focusing on positive things about someone or something that has been bringing up negative emotions is a powerful way to retrain your thoughts. It allows you to attract more of what you actually want from that person or situation with greater ease, rather than more of the same.

This may seem difficult at first, especially with certain people or subjects. However, in spite of how negatively you feel about a co-worker, for example, with some effort you should be able to list at least 6 things about him or her that are good, in your opinion (she's polite to customers, she wears nice clothes, she loves her kids, etc.). Or, your current apartment may be cramped and poorly laid out, but there are still positive characteristics (it's relatively sound-proof, it's in a safe neighborhood, the walls are a nice color, etc.).

Deliberately focusing on the positive aspects of someone or something will also help you retrain your perspective in general. It's also beneficial to focus on the positive aspects of people you love, including yourself, or items such as pens, or bowls, etc.

Example:

Positive aspects of my car:

1. The seats are comfortable.
2. The stereo system sounds great.
3. I love the unusual color.
4. Most of the body is in fine shape.
5. It's always been great on gas.
6. The transmission is new.

Practice writing a Positive Aspects List here. We suggest writing 6 things on each list, and making every day's list different.

Positive aspects of _____:

1. _____
2. _____
3. _____
4. _____
5. _____
6. _____

Meditation/Relaxation

Taking a short time to de-clutter your thoughts will quickly raise your vibration, and you'll release any negative thoughts floating around in your mind.

Find a way to meditate daily for 15 minutes. Sit quietly and focus on your breathing, or play your favorite meditation CD.

Or, try coloring, if meditation doesn't float your boat. We've found, and many seem to agree, that coloring is not only really, really fun, it's also *as beneficial as meditation*. According to clinical psychologist Ben Michaelis, Ph.D., coloring is something he "absolutely supports for mental health," and it's "absolutely another form of meditation."[3] It makes sense. Any time we indulge in something we enjoy, we literally get lost in the fun of it.

Furthermore, coloring can spark creativity, even in those who have never considered themselves creative. Now, we can also use coloring as a way to spark the creation of anything we desire, as we learn to deliberately use the Law of Attraction to our benefit. We suggest that you enjoy coloring the images we've included throughout this Planner using colored pencils or Crayola Twisters (to protect other pages).

---

[3] Why Coloring is a Beneficial Stress Relief, HuffPost Live, July 27, 2015, http://live.huffingtonpost.com/r/segment/coloring-adults-stress/55af7fb1fe34445cec000185

Go Outside

Step outside every day, even for a moment, to appreciate nature and acknowledge Source.

As you stand and take in the beauty of nature around you, say:

"Source, I acknowledge that I am the object of your positive attention, and I appreciate your continual gaze on behalf of my wellbeing.

Today, no matter where I am, no matter what I am doing, and no matter who I am doing it with, I will be consciously aware that you are there with me – appreciating me, guiding me, supporting me, uplifting me, assisting me, acknowledging me, inspiring me, helping me, loving me, aware of me, showing me, and having fun with me!

Thank you Source!" (Inspired by Abraham.)

Here is an Abraham-inspired EFT[+] tapping for use when acknowledging Source, if you wish. If you're not familiar with Emotional Freedom Technique, see page 24 for information.

Eyebrow (near bridge of nose):   ___[fill in your preferred name for Source]___, I acknowledge that I am the object of your positive attention.

Side of Eye: I am appreciating your continual gaze on behalf of my well-being.

Under the Eye: Today, no matter where I am, no matter where I am going,

Under Nose: no matter what I am doing, and no matter who I am doing it with,

Chin: I will be in conscious awareness that you too are there with me,

Collarbone: appreciating me, supporting me, assisting me,

Under Arm: acknowledging me, inspiring me, guiding me,

Crown of Head: having fun with me, acknowledging me, loving me,

Eyebrow (near bridge of nose): inspiring me, helping me, aware of me,

Side of Eye: supporting me, showing me, inspiring me, uplifting me,

Under the Eye: allowing me to create a wonderful, joyous life for myself and with others.

Under Nose: I will love myself and be easy on myself today.

Chin: I will do what is important to get done today, and always make how I feel a priority.

[+] Emotional Freedom Technique.

Collarbone: I will appreciate the contrast life presents me, as well as those I show myself, and immediately focus on what I choose to enjoy instead.

Under Arm: I realize life is a journey, and my goal is to enjoy it.

Crown of Head: I choose to enjoy this journey, have loads of fun, and inspire others to do the same!

Just For Fun

Have FUN every day! Find a way! We can't stress how important this is. As Abraham says, Freedom is the basis of your life, Joy is the purpose of your life, and Growth is the result. That's right, joy is the purpose. Your happiness allows you to create the life you want, so it's your "job" to be happy.

So, make a daily plan to have fun, one way or another. Write it down and commit yourself!

My plan for fun today: _____

_____

More Fantastic and Highly Effective Tools

What I'd Like to Be, Do, or Have

This tool will give you clarity about your desires, and help fuel your Appreciation/Gratitude Intentions Lists. We rarely take the time for serious daydreaming, but it's actually one of the most productive actions we can take, provided we're focused on what we want, and not the lack of it.

Write a list of 16 things you would like to Be, Do, or Have – anything at all. Don't worry about whether they're "realistic" or whether you believe they're even remotely possible. This is your "wish list," so to speak.

If you get stuck, think briefly about something you don't like. Then, identify its opposite and add it to your list. Just remember to keep your list positive, so you can deliberately attract what you wish to Be, Do, or Have, *not the lack of it.*

Examples:

I'd like to:

1. Be more physically fit.
2. Try a new recipe.
3. Have a new outfit.

Practice writing 16 things you want to Be, Do, or Have:

I'd like to:

1. _____   9. _____

2. _____   10. _____

3. _____   11. _____

4. _____   12. _____

5. _____   13. _____

6. _____   14. _____

7. _____   15. _____

8. _____   16. _____

Appreciating the Contrast and Pivoting

Life is like a buffet, as Abraham often suggests. You're faced with a wide variety of choices every day, some of which will please you, and others that won't. It would benefit you greatly to learn to appreciate even the things you don't like, because they give you greater clarity regarding what you want instead.

➤ When you're faced with something unwanted, recognize it as contrast, and appreciate it for making your desires more clear. If the idea of appreciating someone or something that is really pushing your buttons seems hard to swallow, think of the alternative – more of the same!

Also, consider the value of contrast beyond your personal life experience. Abraham said it perfectly: "And so, your exposure to contrast sharpens your focus and gives birth to new preferences and desires. In fact, this valuable contrast assures the eternal expansion of All-That-Is."[5]

➤ Once you've appreciated the contrast, immediately begin focusing on those desires. Tell yourself exactly what you'd rather have instead of whatever you're facing. A great place to start is by telling yourself, "What I want right now is to feel good!" Then, focus on the specifics. Try to find thoughts that make you feel better in that moment, whether they pertain to the contrast that you're presently experiencing or to something completely different, as long as it feels better.

Use the Pivoting Tool as often as it takes for any given subject. Try to pivot as soon as your thoughts about the subject result in any negative emotions at all. Over time, you'll train your thoughts on that subject to vibrate highly enough (positively enough) to match the frequency of what you really want and attract it into your life. In the meantime, pivoting will help you feel better in that moment, and you'll become increasingly aware of your freedom to choose your thoughts and the power they wield.

Examples:

Your child is being very rowdy in the next room, and you're feeling stressed and short-tempered. Your initial thoughts are identifying the contrast, "I don't need this right now! I don't want to have to keep going in there to quiet him down!" Next, you pivot and immediately follow with thoughts like, "Thanks for the contrast, son. I choose to be much more relaxed about this, and I choose to see you playing quietly."

You're making cold calls for work, and someone hangs up on you. At first, you think, "I can't believe she just hung up on me! How rude! I hate it when people act that way." Next, you pivot and think, "I appreciate the contrast she just gave me. I choose to call people who are respectful, and who are a match to the products I offer."

---

[5] Esther and Jerry Hicks, *Ask and It Is Given: The Teachings of Abraham* (Hay House, 2004), 189.

Primary Focus

The Primary Focus tool will help you break your projects down into smaller steps so you can feel more at ease and in control as you move towards attaining your goal.

We've included this tool as part of each Project Plan (see page 69), along with the What, Why, Why tool and the Writing Your Script tool, to help you sharpen your focus and get you vibrating highly enough (positively enough) to match the frequency of your desired outcome, in order to attract it in your life.

Don't forget – Deliberate Planning is useful for anything you want to give positive momentum to --

- ➢ Organizing the events of a day
- ➢ Dealing with upcoming projects with many steps
- ➢ Major life events such as moving, finding a new job, or planning a wedding
- ➢ Deliberately attracting anything you want to be, do, or have into your reality

While it's important for you to ultimately attain your desired outcome, remember that the biggest goal is to enjoy *every step* of the way. In other words, enjoy the journey!

Example:

Primary Focus

Desired Outcome: To move into a new apartment by August 1, 2016.

Date: June 1, 2016

Primary Focus Steps	Step-by-Step Focus
1. Find a new 3-bedroom apartment.	1. Figure out how much rent we can afford. 2. Determine location of new home. 3. Contact local realtor. 4. Let friends know we're looking for a new place. 5. Check craigslist ads.
2. Purge for move.	1. Go through each room and separate items – keep only what we need or love. 2. Purge bedrooms – one a day. 3. Purge kitchen in one day. 4. Purge living room and dining room in one day. 5. Donate items and plan tag sale.

Practice completing the **Primary Focus portion** of an upcoming Project Plan:

Primary Focus

Desired Outcome: _____

Date: _____

Primary Focus Steps	Step-by-Step Focus
1.	1.
	2.
	3.
	4.
	5.
	6.
2.	1.
	2.
	3.
	4.
	5.
	6.
3.	1.
	2.
	3.
	4.
	5.
	6.

What, Why, Why

Once you know **what** you want, this tool provides an easy way to improve your thoughts about it and ultimately attract it into your life.

First, write down what you want. Keep it simple and brief.

Next, list all the reasons why you want it, making sure that each reason is worded as a positive statement. In other words, rather than writing "I don't want to be abused any longer," write something like "It feels great to be treated with respect" (see next tool for further description).

It's very important to use positive "feeling" words in this list. Imagine all the good feelings you will experience when you have what you want, and list every one you can possibly think of!

Finally, list reasons why you know you already have what you want, why it's already part of your reality. This is where you acknowledge all the "work" you're doing by using these tools to raise your vibration. Give yourself credit! You're a deliberate planner! Write down why you know you've attained your goal with ease.

Then, use what you've written to fuel your daily Appreciation/Gratitude Intentions Lists, or for Writing Your Script (see page 20).

Example:

> ➤ <u>What I Want</u>: I want my body to be fit, and at a healthy weight for my height.
> ➤ <u>Why I Want It</u>:
>> 1. I'll feel so comfortable in my clothes.
>> 2. It'll feel so good to move around with ease, and be physically active again.
>> 3. I look forward to hiking more in the woods, which always gives me a wonderful feeling of peace and appreciation for the beauty around me.
>> 4. It will feel great spending my money on new clothes. I will love clothes shopping!
>> 5. I'll feel a sense of pride in my ability to do more things around my house independently.
>> 6. I will really appreciate the fun and freedom I'll have choosing from a huge selection of wonderful clothes.
>
> ➤ <u>Why I Already Have It</u>:
>> 1. I know I'm a powerful creator, and that I'm getting better and better at doing it deliberately.
>> 2. I'm making daily lists of the positive aspects of my body – there are many, when I really think about it!
>> 3. I spend time every day visualizing myself having fun shopping for new clothes at my ideal weight.

4. I also visualize my body releasing excess calories with ease, and my muscles working effortlessly.

5. I eat what I want, when I want it, as long as it feels like a "Hell yes!" to me at that moment. I pay close attention to my emotions, because I know they guide me towards my desired outcome when they're positive.

6. I use the Segment Intending tool often, to pre-pave different segments of my day, just before each one begins.

Practice using the What, Why, Why tool:

<u>What I Want:</u> _____

<u>Why I Want It:</u>

1. _____

2. _____

3. _____

4. _____

5. _____

6. _____

<u>Why I Know I Already Have It:</u>

1. _____

2. _____

3. _____

4. _____

5. _____

6. _____

<u>Making Positive Statements</u>

You probably know people who always complain about their numerous health issues, or persistent lack of money, or a series of unhappy relationships. Most call them unlucky. We and many others now know, however, that these folks have unwittingly attracted more and more of what they didn't want "merely" by talking to others about their problems, and thinking about them, over and over again.

If you focus primarily on negativity, the Law of Attraction will work to bring you more to feel badly about. So, if you say, "I'm sick of being broke," you're setting yourself up for more situations that match that negative vibration, and will provide more of that negative feeling.

Wouldn't it feel better to say, "I choose to be financially secure and at ease?" Try focusing more positively with your statements, and watch what happens. This takes a lot of practice at first (written reminders may help) because, as with the Appreciation/Gratitude Intentions List, it may feel too much like pretending and therefore not effective. But it is *quite* effective and, in our opinion, one of the most important tools you can use. The *positive* feeling behind these statements is extremely important; if you feel any angst when you state them, you're actually pushing your desire away.

Remind yourself that you are a powerful creator, that you are in complete control of your reality, and that you're learning to take charge of your future deliberately.

Segment Intending

When you're already feeling pretty well, this is a great process to use during both the planning and implementation stages of your projects, and throughout your day. Abraham describes it as follows:

> It is the process whereby you define the vibrational characteristics of the time segment you are moving into. It is a way of pre-paving your vibrational path, so to speak, for easier and more enjoyable travel.[6]

In other words, you can set the desired tone for each new segment of your day, or for an upcoming segment in your more distant future, by focusing specifically on the way you want it to turn out. This tool works wonderfully, because it limits the overwhelment and confusion you experience when you try to consider everything at the same time.

Examples:

> "I know that, for the next several minutes, I'm going to be able to happily sit down and write out my plan for getting my house ready for company in 2 weeks. It's going to be easy to think of all the steps, and it's going to feel great getting them all organized. Then, I'll feel like I'm in complete control, which I am!"

---

[6] Esther and Jerry Hicks, *Ask and It Is Given: The Teachings of Abraham* (Hay House, 2004), 165.

"I intend to have a wonderful time, over the next 2 weeks, watching my house look better and better! It's going to be so much easier attacking it with a plan I feel good about, and I know it's all going to come together beautifully!"

"I see this phone call I'm about to make being a piece of cake. I'm going to be able to speak clearly and with ease, and enjoy the conversation. I know that I'm the one who chooses my thoughts, and I choose to think only good thoughts during the call."

Writing Your Script

Tell your story the way you choose it to be. You're writing a play about what it's going to be like when you get your desired outcome, but using the present tense, as if it's already happened and you're living it. Use this Planner, a journal, or even a Powerpoint presentation including images and other media.

Incorporate all 6 of your senses (sight, taste, touch, smell, hearing, *and emotions*) into your story, and go into as much detail as possible.

Emphasize the way each delicious detail makes you feel! Milk the emotions – you want your audience (you) to really *feel the feelings* while reading your script.

Afterwards, spend about 5 minutes visualizing having attained what you want. Sit quietly, eyes closed, and go through the entire scene in your mind, imagining yourself living the experience right now.

This is a very powerful tool to retrain your focus and raise your vibration to match your desires.

Example:

Suppose you want a new BMW. You might write something like this:

I'm so excited, as I walk out of the grocery store and spot my brand new, beautiful, white BMW glimmering in the sunlight. The warm sun on my back feels so good as I almost sprint towards the car.

As I move the shopping bags around on the white leather back seat, I smile at how smooth it feels on the back of my hand. I love the sound the door makes as I close it – that "solid," well-built sound.

I settle into the comfortable driver's seat and relax, taking in that glorious "new car smell" for a few moments before turning the key. I can hardly hear it running, the engine is so quiet. Suddenly, I notice the cool breeze of the A/C on my face.

I back out using the rear view camera that I appreciate soooo much, and smile as I think about how easy it is to maneuver this car. As I pull up to the street, waiting for traffic to clear, I take a few sips of the delicious, refreshing cold water I just bought. I'm really enjoying the cold, thirst-quenching satisfaction I'm getting from it on this hot day.

I'm feeling so content and happy! I knew I'd get my dream car. After I drop my groceries off, I'm heading out for a road trip!!

Practice writing a script here. Pick any subject, and just have fun!

_____

_____

_____

_____

_____

_____

_____

_____

_____

_____

_____

_____

_____

_____

_____

_____

_____

Placemat Process

If you're feeling overwhelmed, take a piece of paper and draw a line down the middle (we've included some blanks beginning on page 91).

On the left side, write "Things I Will Do." List below 3-4 things you choose to take responsibility for, and mean it. Only include things you know you can reasonably do, and are determined to do.

On the right side, write "Things I'd Like the Universe to Take Care Of." List *everything else* on that side of the page.

According to Abraham, this is "the most powerful process for gaining access to the leverage of energy, the power of the Universe."[7] This is because you are focusing your desires, *and* doing it in a less resistant way than you have before, by giving everything else to the Universe.

Then, you will find that you were able to accomplish the items on your list with ease, and you'll feel great for having done them. Many of the things on the Universe's side of the page will resolve themselves, now that you've let go of your old belief that *you had to do them, but didn't have enough time.*[8] This tool can be used on a daily basis, or just whenever you're a match to it. Feel free to copy the blank Placemat at the back of the book.

Example:

Things I Will Do	Things I'd Like the Universe to Take Care Of
1. Mow lawn. 2. Laundry. 3. Call sister. 4. Go for a walk.	1. Enable me to attract enough money to take care of my bills and feel at peace. 2. Allow me to organize my files with ease. 3. Allow my husband to be more patient with our children. 4. Send me 5 new clients this month that I can handle with ease. 5. Help me easily find an outfit for the wedding.

Practice using the Placemat Process on the next page:

---

[7] Abraham-Hicks Publications, Boca Raton Workshop, http://www.abraham-hicks.com, (March 7, 2013).
[8] Ibid.

Things I Will Do	Things I'd Like the Universe to Take Care Of

Emotional Freedom Technique (EFT)[2]

Use this tool to get past limiting beliefs and negativity. You'll gain confidence and be able to act with greater ease, as you become a more deliberate planner. Releasing negativity will allow you to more easily recognize and receive Universal "nudges" toward the actions that will bring you closer to your desired outcomes. As a result of using EFT, you will feel better which will, as Abraham states, make you an emotional match to your desires.

EFT is based on the premise that negative emotions result from a disruption in the body's energy system. Like acupuncture, it utilizes the body's energy meridians to activate healing and restore balance (without the needles).

Tapping on a sequence of acupressure points can "collapse" feelings such as guilt, resentment, anger, fear, and anxiety so that they no longer affect you.

Physical issues can also be improved using EFT.

The location of the Tapping Points are shown in the illustration below.

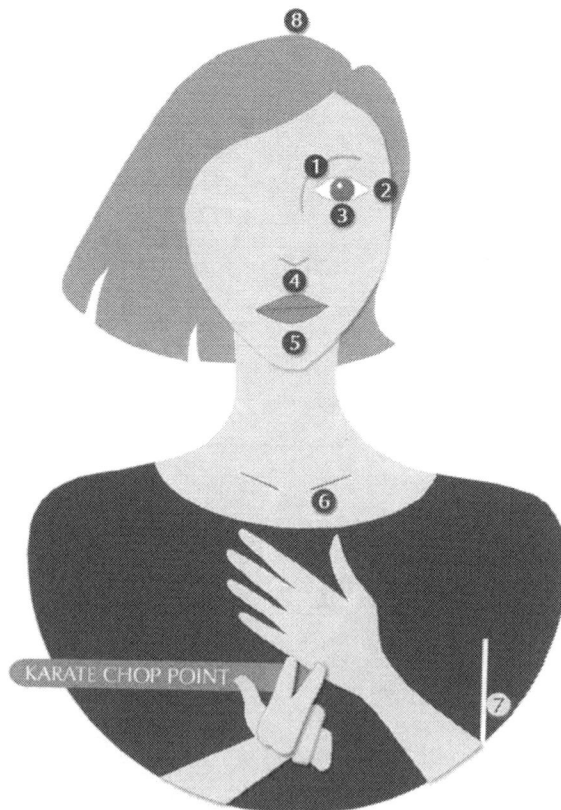

(1) Eyebrow (at nose)   (3) Under Eye   (5) Chin   (7) Under Arm
(2) Side of Eye   (4) Under Nose   (6) Collarbone   (8) Crown of Head

---

[2] Emotional Freedom Technique was developed by Gary Craig. See www.emofree.com for further information.

Following the order in the Tapping you choose, tap each point lightly with two or more fingertips approximately 7 times (using either hand), while saying the accompanying tapping statement aloud.

Karate Chop Point: located in the soft, fleshy side of your palm between the base of your pinky finger and your wrist. This point is sometimes used for the EFT Setup Statement.

Eyebrow: located at the beginning of your eyebrow, just up and over from the bridge of your nose.

Side of Eye: located at outside corner of your eye, on the bony ridge.

Under Eye: located on bone underneath your eye, directly under the pupil.

Under Nose: located just under your nose, in the little crevice above your upper lip.

Chin: located just under your bottom lip, in the depression between your lip and chin.

Collarbone: located next to the depression at the base of your throat, directly below the collarbone.

Under Arm: located on side of your body, about 4 inches directly below your armpit.

Crown of Head: located on the top of your head.

Here is a Daily Tapping for Joy:

Eyebrow: I am energized and excited about today. I use Law of Attraction tools every morning to build up positive momentum, making me a match to wonderful opportunities and outcomes.

Side of Eye: I understand that I get what I focus on, so I am focused on being happy and at ease.

Under Eye: It feels great starting off my day feeling happy. I intentionally focus positively as soon as I awaken.

Under Nose: I complete the things that are important to get done, and take time for fun.

Chin: I value and appreciate all that I am. It's empowering to know that I'm in charge of how I feel and what I attract.

Collarbone: I am grateful for my patience and acceptance of others. I appreciate the contrast life shows me, and I focus on how I'd like to feel and what I'd like to experience.

Under Arm: I take responsibility for myself. I nurture myself daily, and have fun.

Crown of Head: I know that nothing is more important than lining up my energy and feeling good. No matter what, I am enough, and I'm always in the process of expanding to become more. I love knowing I am Source and hold the power that creates worlds.

Here is a Tapping for Motivation and Ease in Attracting Positive Outcomes:

Karate Chop Point (while tapping, repeat 3 times): Even though sometimes attaining goals has been difficult for me, I love and accept myself. Even though I just can't seem to get started moving towards completing this project (or step), I love and accept myself. Even though sometimes I get really frustrated with myself because I am procrastinating so much, I love and accept myself.

Eyebrow: I'm frustrated because I know completing this project (or step) will feel good to me, but I'm not doing anything about attracting the outcome I desire.

Side of Eye: It's frustrating when I keep doing the same thing over and over again – being slow about making progress.

Under Eye: Abraham says we're not procrastinating, we're lining up our energy.

Under Nose: Lining up my energy prior to taking action seems to makes any action I take much more productive.

Chin: I need to be easy about all of this; I'll never get it all done anyway.

Collarbone: What if it was easy for me to use the tools here that feel good to me. The most important thing is that I feel good, and then everything will fall into place. I will be more aware of Universal nudges when I'm feeling good. It will be easy for me to take inspired action, and to get closer to feeling my goal coming into fruition.

Under Arm: Everything is always working out for me. I'm never going to get it all done, so I'm going to focus on having fun with this.

Crown of Head: I love this tapping, it makes everything feel so much clearer to me. I feel much better lining up my energy first thing in the morning and maintaining positive momentum longer and longer throughout my day. I love the anticipation and fun of attaining and attracting my goals with greater ease. I love focusing on the reasons why I will feel even better attaining this goal. I can visualize how awesome it will be. I know this will be easy!

Here is a Tapping for Feeling Calm:

Karate Chop Point (while tapping, repeat 3 times): Even though I feel so stressed because _____

_____, I love and accept myself.

Eyebrow: I feel so stressed I can hardly think straight.

Side of Eye: When I feel this stressed, I don't know what to do next!

Under Eye: I don't feel like doing anything. Even if I tried, I don't think I would be very productive right now.

Under Nose: There is so much I wanted to do today, but nothing seems to be going right.

Chin: The more I focus on how stressed I am, the more stressed I feel. I've had enough of this.

Collarbone: What if it was easy for me to just think more generally. I've been stressed like this before and ended up okay. Everyone has some tough days. I came forth to experience contrast and expand my preferences – that's what makes me eternal. I guess I'm on the right track, because this is a great contrast for me. Now, I know exactly what I want – to feel calmer and more in control. I'm feeling better already.

Under Arm: I'm just going to be easy with myself. There is plenty of time to get things done. It just might not be today, and that's okay.

Crown of Head: I can do just what I need to do today, and everything else can wait. There have been plenty of days when I was extremely productive, and a lot of things fell right into place for me. It will be okay; I really feel better already. I can feel my body relaxing. My mind is more at ease, too.

Manifestation Board

Use the blank pages that follow to create Manifestation Boards, where you can glue images or words that depict the joy of having attracted your desired outcomes.

Example:

PAMELA THOMPSON AND DONNA HAWKINS   29

Celebrate Your Successes!

Reflecting on past successes is a very effective way to face challenging new desires and goals. It reminds you just how powerful a creator you really are, and helps you create new beliefs about attracting your desires with ease. It's an awesome way to validate yourself, while increasing your self-confidence.

Make a list of your past successes, big and small – include anything that makes you feel good. List projects you've completed with ease, things you've become good at, accomplishments you're proud of, different or unexpected ways money has come into your life, all the great relationships you have, the perfect outfit you just found, and so on. Add to your list, or begin a new one, any time. We've provided a page at the end of the book that you may copy for future use.

Start giving yourself credit for all the good things in your life – you've successfully attracted a lot to celebrate! Now, start using the power of your past successes to quickly and easily build momentum towards attracting your new desires and outcomes.

We recommend re-reading your list every morning and every night, as long as it feels good to do so. At first, this may seem weird to do, but the more you do it, the more successful you will be. As Jerry Hicks used to say, "The better it gets, the better it gets, the better it gets." It's true!

Example:

Celebrating My Successes!

1. I'm a wonderful parent.
2. I provide a clean, happy home for my family.
3. I'm a good friend, and have many friends.
4. I got a promotion last year at work.
5. I'm a responsible pet owner.
6. I received an unexpected 40% rebate on the lawn mower I bought last month.
7. I'm now an excellent public speaker.
8. I planned a great vacation to California.
9. I've become very well-organized.
10. I'm a fantastic baker.
11. I passed my real estate test.
12. I finished my tax returns before the deadline with amazing ease.

Use the next page to start celebrating!

Celebrating My Successes!

1. _____

2. _____

3. _____

4. _____

5. _____

6. _____

7. _____

8. _____

9. _____

10. _____

11. _____

12. _____

13. _____

14. _____

15. _____

16. _____

17. _____

18. _____

19. _____

20. _____

21. _____

22. _____

23. _____

24. _____

68 Seconds of Pure Positive Focus

If there are areas of your life that have provided you with long-term contrast, you've built up quite a lot of *vibrational momentum* towards more of the same. Here's an effective way to turn that momentum around and head towards what you want instead.

Identify something in your life right now that makes you feel really good when you think about it – something that's really working well or something you deeply appreciate – and use it to practice raising the frequency at which your thoughts are vibrating. If you can focus on this easy feeling subject for 17 seconds, and then another 17 seconds, and another, and another – for a total of 68 seconds – you will have achieved vibrational momentum in the right direction.

If you repeat this pure positive focus daily (or more) for 30 days, you will have raised your *most practiced frequency* sufficiently to allow your desired outcomes in other areas. According to Abraham, this daily focus is powerfully effective because *practice and momentum are intertwined.*[10]

You can choose one subject to focus on for 30 days, write about it for at least 68 seconds, and *simply re-read it daily.* It doesn't matter what format you use to write – try scripting, or writing a letter, or making bullet lists of positive aspects – whatever "raises your cork," as Abraham likes to say.

Or, you can write for 68 seconds daily, choosing from a variety of subjects you feel good about. It's all about getting consistent practice keeping your vibrational momentum going in the direction of your desires!

Example:

I really love the way my house faces every direction. I can see gorgeous sunsets, and get sunlight through key windows at the right times. I love the heating system, and plumbing, and foundation! I especially appreciate my running water! I love my wood floors, and old fashioned bathroom. I really like the color green on the outside – it blends well with the woods around it. I love the layout of the rooms, and the detached garage. I love my drapes and rugs, and how well they go with everything and how much they help with heat efficiency. I love the fact that the inside stays nice and comfortable, even on the hottest days.

Use the next page to start your 68 Seconds! You can probably fit more than one day's 68 Second Focus on a page – it doesn't take very long.

There are 8 lined pages in the back (see page 99) for your pure positive focus.

---

[10] Abraham-Hicks Publications, unknown Workshop, https://www.youtube.com/watch?v=VPoGeW-lqWc (date and location unkown).

ONE MONTH TO POSITIVE OUTCOMES [11]

Using the Daily Tools beginning on page 5 for one month will greatly enhance your ability to match the high frequency of your desired outcomes with ease. We have provided the following pages for that purpose.

We cannot stress enough how important it is that you complete the pages every day. Writing is the greatest vehicle you have for establishing and maintaining the focus of your thoughts, and it's the most effective way to increase your vibration and improve your perspective about the outcomes you want.

If you knew that your thoughts were powerful,

and you knew that your words were even more powerful,

and if you knew that writing something down is more powerful still,

and if you knew that when you write it that the Universe would go to work

immediatey to begin bringing it to you,

wouldn't you want to find something RIGHT NOW to write with?

Where oh where would one find such a thing?

Our love,
Jerry & Esther [12]

---

[11] We've included an additional blank Daily Tools page at the back – feel free to copy.

[12] Abraham-Hicks Caribbean Cruise, unknown date. Esther and Jerry left this quote from Abraham in each attendee's cabin, to accompany a gift of a journal and a pen.

Date: _____

Today's Appreciation/Gratitude List

Today, I really appreciate:

1. _____
2. _____
3. _____
4. _____
5. _____
6. _____

Today's Positive Aspects List

Positive aspects of _____ :

1. _____
2. _____
3. _____
4. _____
5. _____
6. _____

Today's Appreciation/Gratitude Intentions List

Today, I really appreciate:

1. _____
2. _____
3. _____
4. _____
5. _____
6. _____

Today's Meditation or Relaxation

How do I plan to meditate or relax today? _____

Today's Go Outside

When do I plan to step outdoors and acknowledge Source and all of nature? _____

Today's Just for Fun

How will I have FUN today? _____

Date: _____

Today's Appreciation/Gratitude List

Today, I really appreciate:

1. _____
2. _____
3. _____
4. _____
5. _____
6. _____

Today's Positive Aspects List

Positive aspects of _____:

1. _____
2. _____
3. _____
4. _____
5. _____
6. _____

Today's Appreciation/Gratitude Intentions List

Today, I really appreciate:

1. _____
2. _____
3. _____
4. _____
5. _____
6. _____

Today's Meditation or Relaxation

How do I plan to meditate or relax today? _____

Today's Go Outside

When do I plan to step outdoors and acknowledge Source and all of nature? _____

Today's Just for Fun

How will I have FUN today? _____

Date: _____

Today's Appreciation/Gratitude List

Today, I really appreciate:

1. _____

2. _____

3. _____

4. _____

5. _____

6. _____

Today's Positive Aspects List

Positive aspects of _____:

1. _____

2. _____

3. _____

4. _____

5. _____

6. _____

Today's Appreciation/Gratitude Intentions List

Today, I really appreciate:

1. _____

2. _____

3. _____

4. _____

5. _____

6. _____

Today's Meditation or Relaxation

How do I plan to meditate or relax today? _____

Today's Go Outside

When do I plan to step outdoors and acknowledge Source and all of nature? _____

Today's Just for Fun

How will I have FUN today? _____

Date: _____

Today's Appreciation/Gratitude List

Today, I really appreciate:

1. _____
2. _____
3. _____
4. _____
5. _____
6. _____

Today's Positive Aspects List

Positive aspects of _____:

1. _____
2. _____
3. _____
4. _____
5. _____
6. _____

Today's Appreciation/Gratitude Intentions List

Today, I really appreciate:

1. _____
2. _____
3. _____
4. _____
5. _____
6. _____

Today's Meditation or Relaxation

How do I plan to meditate or relax today? _____

Today's Go Outside

When do I plan to step outdoors and acknowledge Source and all of nature? _____

Today's Just for Fun

How will I have FUN today? _____

Date: _____

Today's Appreciation/Gratitude List

Today, I really appreciate:

1. _____
2. _____
3. _____
4. _____
5. _____
6. _____

Today's Positive Aspects List

Positive aspects of _____:

1. _____
2. _____
3. _____
4. _____
5. _____
6. _____

Today's Appreciation/Gratitude Intentions List

Today, I really appreciate:

1. _____
2. _____
3. _____
4. _____
5. _____
6. _____

Today's Meditation or Relaxation

How do I plan to meditate or relax today? _____

Today's Go Outside

When do I plan to step outdoors and acknowledge Source and all of nature? _____

Today's Just for Fun

How will I have FUN today? _____

Date: _____

Today's Appreciation/Gratitude List

Today, I really appreciate:

1. _____
2. _____
3. _____
4. _____
5. _____
6. _____

Today's Positive Aspects List

Positive aspects of _____:

1. _____
2. _____
3. _____
4. _____
5. _____
6. _____

Today's Appreciation/Gratitude Intentions List

Today, I really appreciate:

1. _____
2. _____
3. _____
4. _____
5. _____
6. _____

Today's Meditation or Relaxation

How do I plan to meditate or relax today? _____

Today's Go Outside

When do I plan to step outdoors and acknowledge Source and all of nature? _____

Today's Just for Fun

How will I have FUN today? _____

Date: _____

Today's Appreciation/Gratitude List

Today, I really appreciate:

1. _____
2. _____
3. _____
4. _____
5. _____
6. _____

Today's Positive Aspects List

Positive aspects of _____ :

1. _____
2. _____
3. _____
4. _____
5. _____
6. _____

Today's Appreciation/Gratitude Intentions List

Today, I really appreciate:

1. _____
2. _____
3. _____
4. _____
5. _____
6. _____

Today's Meditation or Relaxation

How do I plan to meditate or relax today? _____

Today's Go Outside

When do I plan to step outdoors and acknowledge Source and all of nature? _____

Today's Just for Fun

How will I have FUN today? _____

Date: _____

Today's Appreciation/Gratitude List

Today, I really appreciate:

1. _____
2. _____
3. _____
4. _____
5. _____
6. _____

Today's Positive Aspects List

Positive aspects of _____:

1. _____
2. _____
3. _____
4. _____
5. _____
6. _____

Today's Appreciation/Gratitude Intentions List

Today, I really appreciate:

1. _____
2. _____
3. _____
4. _____
5. _____
6. _____

Today's Meditation or Relaxation

How do I plan to meditate or relax today? _____

Today's Go Outside

When do I plan to step outdoors and acknowledge Source and all of nature? _____

Today's Just for Fun

How will I have FUN today? _____

Read Celebrating My Successes page every a.m. and p.m.

Date: _____

Today's Appreciation/Gratitude List

Today, I really appreciate:

1. _____
2. _____
3. _____
4. _____
5. _____
6. _____

Today's Positive Aspects List

Positive aspects of _____:

1. _____
2. _____
3. _____
4. _____
5. _____
6. _____

Today's Appreciation/Gratitude Intentions List

Today, I really appreciate:

1. _____
2. _____
3. _____
4. _____
5. _____
6. _____

Today's Meditation or Relaxation

How do I plan to meditate or relax today? _____

Today's Go Outside

When do I plan to step outdoors and acknowledge Source and all of nature? _____

Today's Just for Fun

How will I have FUN today? _____

Date: _____

Today's Appreciation/Gratitude List

Today, I really appreciate:

1. _____
2. _____
3. _____
4. _____
5. _____
6. _____

Today's Positive Aspects List

Positive aspects of _____:

1. _____
2. _____
3. _____
4. _____
5. _____
6. _____

Today's Appreciation/Gratitude Intentions List

Today, I really appreciate:

1. _____
2. _____
3. _____
4. _____
5. _____
6. _____

Today's Meditation or Relaxation

How do I plan to meditate or relax today? _____

Today's Go Outside

When do I plan to step outdoors and acknowledge Source and all of nature? _____

Today's Just for Fun

How will I have FUN today? _____

Date: _____

Today's Appreciation/Gratitude List

Today, I really appreciate:

1. _____

2. _____

3. _____

4. _____

5. _____

6. _____

Today's Positive Aspects List

Positive aspects of _____ :

1. _____

2. _____

3. _____

4. _____

5. _____

6. _____

Today's Appreciation/Gratitude Intentions List

Today, I really appreciate:

1. _____

2. _____

3. _____

4. _____

5. _____

6. _____

Today's Meditation or Relaxation

How do I plan to meditate or relax today? _____

Today's Go Outside

When do I plan to step outdoors and acknowledge Source and all of nature? _____

Today's Just for Fun

How will I have FUN today? _____

Date: _____

Today's Appreciation/Gratitude List

Today, I really appreciate:

1. _____
2. _____
3. _____
4. _____
5. _____
6. _____

Today's Positive Aspects List

Positive aspects of _____:

1. _____
2. _____
3. _____
4. _____
5. _____
6. _____

Today's Appreciation/Gratitude Intentions List

Today, I really appreciate:

1. _____
2. _____
3. _____
4. _____
5. _____
6. _____

Today's Meditation or Relaxation

How do I plan to meditate or relax today? _____

Today's Go Outside

When do I plan to step outdoors and acknowledge Source and all of nature? _____

Today's Just for Fun

How will I have FUN today? _____

Date: _____

Today's Appreciation/Gratitude List

Today, I really appreciate:

1. _____
2. _____
3. _____
4. _____
5. _____
6. _____

Today's Positive Aspects List

Positive aspects of _____:

1. _____
2. _____
3. _____
4. _____
5. _____
6. _____

Today's Appreciation/Gratitude Intentions List

Today, I really appreciate:

1. _____
2. _____
3. _____
4. _____
5. _____
6. _____

Today's Meditation or Relaxation

How do I plan to meditate or relax today? _____

Today's Go Outside

When do I plan to step outdoors and acknowledge Source and all of nature? _____

Today's Just for Fun

How will I have FUN today? _____

Date: _____

Today's Appreciation/Gratitude List

Today, I really appreciate:

1. _____

2. _____

3. _____

4. _____

5. _____

6. _____

Today's Positive Aspects List

Positive aspects of _____:

1. _____

2. _____

3. _____

4. _____

5. _____

6. _____

Today's Appreciation/Gratitude Intentions List

Today, I really appreciate:

1. _____

2. _____

3. _____

4. _____

5. _____

6. _____

Today's Meditation or Relaxation

How do I plan to meditate or relax today? _____

Today's Go Outside

When do I plan to step outdoors and acknowledge Source and all of nature? _____

Today's Just for Fun

How will I have FUN today? _____

Date: _____

Today's Appreciation/Gratitude List

Today, I really appreciate:

1. _____

2. _____

3. _____

4. _____

5. _____

6. _____

Today's Positive Aspects List

Positive aspects of _____:

1. _____

2. _____

3. _____

4. _____

5. _____

6. _____

Today's Appreciation/Gratitude Intentions List

Today, I really appreciate:

1. _____

2. _____

3. _____

4. _____

5. _____

6. _____

Today's Meditation or Relaxation

How do I plan to meditate or relax today? _____

Today's Go Outside

When do I plan to step outdoors and acknowledge Source and all of nature? _____

Today's Just for Fun

How will I have FUN today? _____

Date: _____

Today's Appreciation/Gratitude List

Today, I really appreciate:

1. _____
2. _____
3. _____
4. _____
5. _____
6. _____

Today's Positive Aspects List

Positive aspects of _____:

1. _____
2. _____
3. _____
4. _____
5. _____
6. _____

Today's Appreciation/Gratitude Intentions List

Today, I really appreciate:

1. _____
2. _____
3. _____
4. _____
5. _____
6. _____

Today's Meditation or Relaxation

How do I plan to meditate or relax today? _____

Today's Go Outside

When do I plan to step outdoors and acknowledge Source and all of nature? _____

Today's Just for Fun

How will I have FUN today? _____

Date: _____

Today's Appreciation/Gratitude List

Today, I really appreciate:

1. _____

2. _____

3. _____

4. _____

5. _____

6. _____

Today's Positive Aspects List

Positive aspects of _____:

1. _____

2. _____

3. _____

4. _____

5. _____

6. _____

Today's Appreciation/Gratitude Intentions List

Today, I really appreciate:

1. _____

2. _____

3. _____

4. _____

5. _____

6. _____

Today's Meditation or Relaxation

How do I plan to meditate or relax today? _____

Today's Go Outside

When do I plan to step outdoors and acknowledge Source and all of nature? _____

Today's Just for Fun

How will I have FUN today? _____

Date: _____

Today's Appreciation/Gratitude List

Today, I really appreciate:

1. _____
2. _____
3. _____
4. _____
5. _____
6. _____

Today's Positive Aspects List

Positive aspects of _____:

1. _____
2. _____
3. _____
4. _____
5. _____
6. _____

Today's Appreciation/Gratitude Intentions List

Today, I really appreciate:

1. _____
2. _____
3. _____
4. _____
5. _____
6. _____

Today's Meditation or Relaxation

How do I plan to meditate or relax today? _____

Today's Go Outside

When do I plan to step outdoors and acknowledge Source and all of nature? _____

Today's Just for Fun

How will I have FUN today? _____

Date: _____

Today's Appreciation/Gratitude List

Today, I really appreciate:

1. _____

2. _____

3. _____

4. _____

5. _____

6. _____

Today's Positive Aspects List

Positive aspects of _____:

1. _____

2. _____

3. _____

4. _____

5. _____

6. _____

Today's Appreciation/Gratitude Intentions List

Today, I really appreciate:

1. _____

2. _____

3. _____

4. _____

5. _____

6. _____

Today's Meditation or Relaxation

How do I plan to meditate or relax today? _____

Today's Go Outside

When do I plan to step outdoors and acknowledge Source and all of nature? _____

Today's Just for Fun

How will I have FUN today? _____

Date: _____

Today's Appreciation/Gratitude List

Today, I really appreciate:

1. _____
2. _____
3. _____
4. _____
5. _____
6. _____

Today's Positive Aspects List

Positive aspects of _____:

1. _____
2. _____
3. _____
4. _____
5. _____
6. _____

Today's Appreciation/Gratitude Intentions List

Today, I really appreciate:

1. _____
2. _____
3. _____
4. _____
5. _____
6. _____

Today's Meditation or Relaxation

How do I plan to meditate or relax today? _____

Today's Go Outside

When do I plan to step outdoors and acknowledge Source and all of nature? _____

Today's Just for Fun

How will I have FUN today? _____

Read Celebrating My Successes page every a.m. and p.m.

Date: _____

Today's Appreciation/Gratitude List

Today, I really appreciate:

1. _____
2. _____
3. _____
4. _____
5. _____
6. _____

Today's Positive Aspects List

Positive aspects of _____:

1. _____
2. _____
3. _____
4. _____
5. _____
6. _____

Today's Appreciation/Gratitude Intentions List

Today, I really appreciate:

1. _____
2. _____
3. _____
4. _____
5. _____
6. _____

Today's Meditation or Relaxation

How do I plan to meditate or relax today? _____

Today's Go Outside

When do I plan to step outdoors and acknowledge Source and all of nature? _____

Today's Just for Fun

How will I have FUN today? _____

Date: _____

Today's Appreciation/Gratitude List

Today, I really appreciate:

1. _____
2. _____
3. _____
4. _____
5. _____
6. _____

Today's Positive Aspects List

Positive aspects of _____:

1. _____
2. _____
3. _____
4. _____
5. _____
6. _____

Today's Appreciation/Gratitude Intentions List

Today, I really appreciate:

1. _____
2. _____
3. _____
4. _____
5. _____
6. _____

Today's Meditation or Relaxation

How do I plan to meditate or relax today? _____

Today's Go Outside

When do I plan to step outdoors and acknowledge Source and all of nature? _____

Today's Just for Fun

How will I have FUN today? _____

Date: _____

Today's Appreciation/Gratitude List

Today, I really appreciate:

1. _____
2. _____
3. _____
4. _____
5. _____
6. _____

Today's Positive Aspects List

Positive aspects of _____ :

1. _____
2. _____
3. _____
4. _____
5. _____
6. _____

Today's Appreciation/Gratitude Intentions List

Today, I really appreciate:

1. _____
2. _____
3. _____
4. _____
5. _____
6. _____

Today's Meditation or Relaxation

How do I plan to meditate or relax today? _____

Today's Go Outside

When do I plan to step outdoors and acknowledge Source and all of nature? _____

Today's Just for Fun

How will I have FUN today? _____

Date: _____

Today's Appreciation/Gratitude List

Today, I really appreciate:

1. _____
2. _____
3. _____
4. _____
5. _____
6. _____

Today's Positive Aspects List

Positive aspects of _____:

1. _____
2. _____
3. _____
4. _____
5. _____
6. _____

Today's Appreciation/Gratitude Intentions List

Today, I really appreciate:

1. _____
2. _____
3. _____
4. _____
5. _____
6. _____

Today's Meditation or Relaxation

How do I plan to meditate or relax today? _____

Today's Go Outside

When do I plan to step outdoors and acknowledge Source and all of nature? _____

Today's Just for Fun

How will I have FUN today? _____

Date: _____

Today's Appreciation/Gratitude List

Today, I really appreciate:

1. _____

2. _____

3. _____

4. _____

5. _____

6. _____

Today's Positive Aspects List

Positive aspects of _____ :

1. _____

2. _____

3. _____

4. _____

5. _____

6. _____

Today's Appreciation/Gratitude Intentions List

Today, I really appreciate:

1. _____

2. _____

3. _____

4. _____

5. _____

6. _____

Today's Meditation or Relaxation

How do I plan to meditate or relax today? _____

Today's Go Outside

When do I plan to step outdoors and acknowledge Source and all of nature? _____

Today's Just for Fun

How will I have FUN today? _____

Date: _____

Today's Appreciation/Gratitude List

Today, I really appreciate:

1. _____
2. _____
3. _____
4. _____
5. _____
6. _____

Today's Positive Aspects List

Positive aspects of _____:

1. _____
2. _____
3. _____
4. _____
5. _____
6. _____

Today's Appreciation/Gratitude Intentions List

Today, I really appreciate:

1. _____
2. _____
3. _____
4. _____
5. _____
6. _____

Today's Meditation or Relaxation

How do I plan to meditate or relax today? _____

Today's Go Outside

When do I plan to step outdoors and acknowledge Source and all of nature? _____

Today's Just for Fun

How will I have FUN today? _____

Date: _____

Today's Appreciation/Gratitude List

Today, I really appreciate:

1. _____
2. _____
3. _____
4. _____
5. _____
6. _____

Today's Positive Aspects List

Positive aspects of _____ :

1. _____
2. _____
3. _____
4. _____
5. _____
6. _____

Today's Appreciation/Gratitude Intentions List

Today, I really appreciate:

1. _____
2. _____
3. _____
4. _____
5. _____
6. _____

Today's Meditation or Relaxation

How do I plan to meditate or relax today? _____

Today's Go Outside

When do I plan to step outdoors and acknowledge Source and all of nature? _____

Today's Just for Fun

How will I have FUN today? _____

Read Celebrating My Successes page every a.m. and p.m.

Date: _____

Today's Appreciation/Gratitude List

Today, I really appreciate:

1. _____
2. _____
3. _____
4. _____
5. _____
6. _____

Today's Positive Aspects List

Positive aspects of _____:

1. _____
2. _____
3. _____
4. _____
5. _____
6. _____

Today's Appreciation/Gratitude Intentions List

Today, I really appreciate:

1. _____
2. _____
3. _____
4. _____
5. _____
6. _____

Today's Meditation or Relaxation

How do I plan to meditate or relax today? _____

Today's Go Outside

When do I plan to step outdoors and acknowledge Source and all of nature? _____

Today's Just for Fun

How will I have FUN today? _____

Date: _____

Today's Appreciation/Gratitude List

Today, I really appreciate:

1. _____

2. _____

3. _____

4. _____

5. _____

6. _____

Today's Positive Aspects List

Positive aspects of _____ :

1. _____

2. _____

3. _____

4. _____

5. _____

6. _____

Today's Appreciation/Gratitude Intentions List

Today, I really appreciate:

1. _____

2. _____

3. _____

4. _____

5. _____

6. _____

Today's Meditation or Relaxation

How do I plan to meditate or relax today? _____

Today's Go Outside

When do I plan to step outdoors and acknowledge Source and all of nature? _____

Today's Just for Fun

How will I have FUN today? _____

Date: _____

Today's Appreciation/Gratitude List

Today, I really appreciate:

1. _____
2. _____
3. _____
4. _____
5. _____
6. _____

Today's Positive Aspects List

Positive aspects of _____ :

1. _____
2. _____
3. _____
4. _____
5. _____
6. _____

Today's Appreciation/Gratitude Intentions List

Today, I really appreciate:

1. _____
2. _____
3. _____
4. _____
5. _____
6. _____

Today's Meditation or Relaxation

How do I plan to meditate or relax today? _____

Today's Go Outside

When do I plan to step outdoors and acknowledge Source and all of nature? _____

Today's Just for Fun

How will I have FUN today? _____

Date: _____

Today's Appreciation/Gratitude List

Today, I really appreciate:

1. _____
2. _____
3. _____
4. _____
5. _____
6. _____

Today's Positive Aspects List

Positive aspects of _____:

1. _____
2. _____
3. _____
4. _____
5. _____
6. _____

Today's Appreciation/Gratitude Intentions List

Today, I really appreciate:

1. _____
2. _____
3. _____
4. _____
5. _____
6. _____

Today's Meditation or Relaxation

How do I plan to meditate or relax today? _____

Today's Go Outside

When do I plan to step outdoors and acknowledge Source and all of nature? _____

Today's Just for Fun

How will I have FUN today? _____

MY PROJECT PLANNER[13]

Remember, this section is for your *Deliberate Planning* – not reactive planning. This is to help you focus your creative energy (literally), and attain your desired outcomes with ease.

When you use the Daily Tools (pages 5-12) in the morning, be sure to include a positive focus on various aspects of the project you're working on. For example, in your Appreciation/Gratitude Intentions List you could focus on a particular project step being completed with ease.

Each Project Plan in the following pages contains 2 sheets, and we've included 12 sets (you can refer to our example on page 15, under Primary Focus, to help you get started).

<u>Primary Focus sheet (Page 1)</u>:

➢ Keep your <u>Desired Outcome</u> clear and concise.

➢ The <u>Primary Focus Steps</u> should include any actions you feel good about taking towards your vision.

➢ Use the <u>Step-by-Step Focus</u> column at the right to add detail to your individual Primary Focus Steps, or to break them down into further steps.

<u>Page 2</u>:

➢ Next, use the <u>What, Why, Why</u> tool to begin to improve your thoughts about attaining your Desired Outcome. (Later, use all your Focus Steps and your What, Why, Why list to fuel subsequent Appreciation/Gratitude Intentions Lists, acting as if you've already attained each one with ease.)

➢ Finally, <u>Write Your Script</u>, and milk every detail of your vision that you can!

This may seem like a lot to do, but the more often you practice raising your vibration and focusing your thoughts and intentions on your Desired Outcomes, the better and faster at it you'll become. Also, it has taken a lifetime for you to develop the habits of thought you currently have regarding various subjects, so you will need to spend some time retraining your perspective.

Then, you will be *amazed* at how quickly the Universe starts to deliver! In other words, once you begin practicing Deliberate Planning, and you have successfully retrained your thoughts, you will *allow* or *attract* your Desired Outcomes with increasing ease!

Note: We've included 8 blank Placemat Process sheets on page 91, in case you'd like to assign some of your Project steps to the Universe!

---

[13] We've included an additional blank set of Project Plan pages at the back – feel free to copy.

Project Plan (p. 1)

Primary Focus

Desired Outcome: _____

Date: _____

Primary Focus Steps	Step-by-Step Focus

Project Plan (p. 2)

<u>What I Want:</u> _____

<u>Why I Want It:</u>

1. _____

2. _____

3. _____

4. _____

5. _____

6. _____

<u>Why I Know I Already Have It:</u>

1. _____

2. _____

3. _____

4. _____

5. _____

6. _____

<u>My Script:</u> _____

_____

_____

_____

_____

_____

_____

_____

_____

_____

Project Plan (p. 1)

Primary Focus

Desired Outcome: _____

Date: _____

Primary Focus Steps	Step-by-Step Focus

Project Plan (p. 2)

Why I Want: _____

Why I Want It:

1. _____
2. _____
3. _____
4. _____
5. _____
6. _____

Why I Know I Already Have It:

1. _____
2. _____
3. _____
4. _____
5. _____
6. _____

My Script: _____

_____

_____

_____

_____

_____

_____

_____

_____

_____

_____

Project Plan (p. 1)

Primary Focus

Desired Outcome: _____

Date: _____

Primary Focus Steps	Step-by-Step Focus

Project Plan (p. 2)

What I Want: _____

Why I Want It:

1. _____

2. _____

3. _____

4. _____

5. _____

6. _____

Why I Know I Already Have It:

1. _____

2. _____

3. _____

4. _____

5. _____

6. _____

My Script: _____

_____

_____

_____

_____

_____

_____

_____

_____

_____

_____

Project Plan (p. 1)

Primary Focus

Desired Outcome: _____

Date: _____

Primary Focus Steps	Step-by-Step Focus

Project Plan (p. 2)

What I Want: _____

Why I Want It:

    1. _____

    2. _____

    3. _____

    4. _____

    5. _____

    6. _____

Why I Know I Already Have It:

    1. _____

    2. _____

    3. _____

    4. _____

    5. _____

    6. _____

My Script: _____

_____

_____

_____

_____

_____

_____

_____

_____

_____

Project Plan (p. 1)

Primary Focus

Desired Outcome: _____

Date: _____

Primary Focus Steps	Step-by-Step Focus

Project Plan (p. 2)

What I Want: _____

Why I Want It:

1. _____

2. _____

3. _____

4. _____

5. _____

6. _____

Why I Know I Already Have It:

1. _____

2. _____

3. _____

4. _____

5. _____

6. _____

My Script: _____

_____

_____

_____

_____

_____

_____

_____

_____

_____

Project Plan (p. 1)

Primary Focus

Desired Outcome: _____

Date: _____

Primary Focus Steps	Step-by-Step Focus

Project Plan (p. 2)

What I Want: _____

Why I Want It:

    1. _____

    2. _____

    3. _____

    4. _____

    5. _____

    6. _____

Why I Know I Already Have It:

    1. _____

    2. _____

    3. _____

    4. _____

    5. _____

    6. _____

My Script: _____

_____

_____

_____

_____

_____

_____

_____

_____

_____

Project Plan (p. 1)

Desired Outcome: _____

Date: _____

Primary Focus Steps	Step-by-Step Focus

Project Plan (p. 2)

What I Want: _____

Why I Want It:

    1. _____

    2. _____

    3. _____

    4. _____

    5. _____

    6. _____

Why I Know I Already Have It:

    1. _____

    2. _____

    3. _____

    4. _____

    5. _____

    6. _____

My Script: _____

_____

_____

_____

_____

_____

_____

_____

_____

_____

Project Plan (p. 1)

Primary Focus

Desired Outcome: _____

Date: _____

Primary Focus Steps	Step-by-Step Focus

Project Plan (p. 2)

__What I Want:__ _____

__Why I Want It:__

    1. _____

    2. _____

    3. _____

    4. _____

    5. _____

    6. _____

__Why I Know I Already Have It:__

    1. _____

    2. _____

    3. _____

    4. _____

    5. _____

    6. _____

__My Script:__ _____

_____

_____

_____

_____

_____

_____

_____

_____

_____

Project Plan (p. 1)

Primary Focus

Desired Outcome: _____

Date: _____

Primary Focus Steps	Step-by-Step Focus

Project Plan (p. 2)

Why I Want: _____

Why I Want It:

    1. _____

    2. _____

    3. _____

    4. _____

    5. _____

    6. _____

Why I Know I Already Have It:

    1. _____

    2. _____

    3. _____

    4. _____

    5. _____

    6. _____

My Script: _____

_____

_____

_____

_____

_____

_____

_____

_____

_____

Project Plan (p. 1)

Primary Focus

Desired Outcome: _____

Date: _____

Primary Focus Steps	Step-by-Step Focus

Project Plan (p. 2)

<u>What I Want:</u> _____

<u>Why I Want It:</u>

    1. _____

    2. _____

    3. _____

    4. _____

    5. _____

    6. _____

<u>Why I Know I Already Have It:</u>

    1. _____

    2. _____

    3. _____

    4. _____

    5. _____

    6. _____

<u>My Script:</u> _____

_____

_____

_____

_____

_____

_____

_____

_____

_____

_____

PLACEMAT PROCESS SHEETS[14]

Things I Will Do	Things I'd Like the Universe to Take Care Of

[14] We've included an additional blank Placemat Process sheet at the back – feel free to copy.

Things I Will Do	Things I'd Like the Universe to Take Care Of

Things I Will Do	Things I'd Like the Universe to Take Care Of

Things I Will Do	Things I'd Like the Universe to Take Care Of

Things I Will Do	Things I'd Like the Universe to Take Care Of

Things I Will Do	Things I'd Like the Universe to Take Care Of

Things I Will Do	Things I'd Like the Universe to Take Care Of

Things I Will Do	Things I'd Like the Universe to Take Care Of

68 SECONDS OF PURE POSITIVE FOCUS[15]

Use these blank lined sheets for 30 days. Remember – write for at least 68 seconds. The longer you write, the more positive momentum you'll build up, so feel free to keep going! After Day 1, you can either:

1. re-read Day 1 daily for 30 days, then skip a line to begin another time for 30 days, or

2. skip a line after the end of Day 1, and write about a new subject to begin Day 2, and so on for 30 days.

Have fun with this tool – it's amazingly powerful!

---

[15] We've included an additional blank 68 Seconds page at the back – feel free to copy.

_____

_____

_____

_____

_____

_____

_____

_____

_____

_____

_____

_____

_____

_____

_____

_____

_____

_____

_____

_____

_____

_____

_____

_____

_____

_____

_____

_____

_____

_____

_____

_____

_____

Additional Coloring Pages

For Fun or Meditation

PAMELA THOMPSON AND DONNA HAWKINS   123

Additional Blank Pages
for Photocopying

Date: _____

Today's Appreciation/Gratitude List

Today, I really appreciate:

1. _____
2. _____
3. _____
4. _____
5. _____
6. _____

Today's Positive Aspects List

Positive aspects of _____ :

1. _____
2. _____
3. _____
4. _____
5. _____
6. _____

Today's Appreciation/Gratitude Intentions List

Today, I really appreciate:

1. _____
2. _____
3. _____
4. _____
5. _____
6. _____

Today's Meditation or Relaxation

How do I plan to meditate or relax today? _____

Today's Go Outside

When do I plan to step outdoors and acknowledge Source and all of nature? _____

Today's Just for Fun

How will I have FUN today? _____

Project Plan (p. 1)

Primary Focus

Desired Outcome: _____

Date: _____

Primary Focus Steps	Step-by-Step Focus

Project Plan (p. 2)

What I Want: _____

Why I Want It:

     1. _____

     2. _____

     3. _____

     4. _____

     5. _____

     6. _____

Why I Know I Already Have It:

     1. _____

     2. _____

     3. _____

     4. _____

     5. _____

     6. _____

My Script: _____

_____

_____

_____

_____

_____

_____

_____

_____

_____

What I'd Like to Be, Do, or Have

I'd like to Be:

1. _____
2. _____
3. _____
4. _____
5. _____
6. _____
7. _____
8. _____

Things I'd like to Do:

1. _____
2. _____
3. _____
4. _____
5. _____
6. _____
7. _____
8. _____

I'd like to Have:

1. _____
2. _____
3. _____
4. _____
5. _____
6. _____
7. _____
8. _____

Placemat Process

Things I Will Do	Things I'd Like the Universe to Take Care Of

Celebrating My Successes! (Read every a.m. and p.m.)

1. _____
2. _____
3. _____
4. _____
5. _____
6. _____
7. _____
8. _____
9. _____
10. _____
11. _____
12. _____
13. _____
14. _____
15. _____
16. _____
17. _____
18. _____
19. _____
20. _____
21. _____
22. _____
23. _____
24. _____

Made in the USA
Lexington, KY
14 March 2018